STORY
THE MENTALITY OF AGENCY

Also by Urrea Jones

On the Nature of Consciousness
The Narrative, a Working Model of Consciousness,
the Cognizable, the Known

Without Stories, There is No Universe, Existence,
Reality, or You

STORY
THE MENTALITY OF
AGENCY

Seizing the Redemptive
Power of Story

Urrea Jones

Cetrict & Wyatt, LLC
cetrictwyattpublications@gmail.com
PO Box 31012, San Francisco, CA 94131

ISBN 979-8-9861620-6-5

Editors: Anthony Wyatt Jones
Barbara Wyatt Jones

Cover Design: Tommy Owen Design, LLC

Printed in the United States of America

Contents

Contents

Contents

STORY
THE MENTALITY OF AGENCY

Prologue

Each of us perceives and experiences our lives as characters in ensembles emulating the plots, ploys and machinations of the scripts of the *Story of Life*.

Nothing can be perceived without a story about it.

Nothing can be experienced except as a story about it.

Our forebears conjured stories that mapped and painted the pathways of the course and meaning of life and created landscapes and dreamscapes that they and we could haunt and inhabit.

Human history spans the millennia travailed by the progenitors as they divined and sculpted the stories that concocted and populated the domain of a survivable reality.

Their conjurings crafted the mental and physical tapestry that is the citadel of our reality, existence and mind.

The reality that we toil within is not a computer-generated or divine labyrinth or simulation.

It is the matrix of the whispers of progenitors that enshrines the landscapes and dreamscapes we live in.

Everything that we perceive and experience is stories concocted by the progenitors.

Their Story of Life (also Story) charts the causeways of life.

Their Story is the panoply of themes, scripts and plots that create the delusion of life as we know it.

We experience life as we emulate and perform the themes, scripts and plots of the progenitors' Story of Life.

We are not pawns caught up in a destiny created and anointed by creators or life forces; rather we are characters trapped in the performance of the progenitors' Story of Life.

We have yet to evolve enough to apprehend a life force, creator or creation that is unsullied by the progenitors' creation stories, even if life forces and creators exist.

We haven't even evolved enough to distill the essence of our own being.

We persist in the myth that the human mind is inscrutable and outside of the reach of understanding because of its infinite variability and complexity.

Nonetheless, it is the progenitors' Story that creates and is the script of the lives that we live.

The performance of their Story gives rise to the experience and drama of daily living.

Our emulation of the progenitors' Story constitutes the reality that we live and experience from birth to death and the places in between.

Our existence, consciousness, reality and self are crystallites formed out of the abyss that cradles and sustains all life.

That abyss was devoid of dimensions, substance and meaning until the progenitors crafted the ark that is the Story of Life.

The Story, like all stories, embodies the themes and plots that capture, organize, script, rationalize, administer and allocate stuff in ways that animate goals, ideations and states.

The story formulation *is the mentality* that conjures our bubble of existence and the experience of living and being.

The story format is analogous to the manuscript paper on which a musical composition is scored.

Stories about stuff imagine, script and animate the experience of it.

Life as we know it would not exist without the Story.

Our lives are experienced as characters in ensembles performing the dramas of the Story of Life.

* * *

What is the Mentality of Agency?

An Agency Mentality requires embracing the likelihood that all of existence, as we know it, is our journey down the storylines of the scripts, plots and venues that are the pathways of our lives.

Our existence was not created and staged by creators or life forces that exist outside of the bubble of the Story, even if we are a parcel of "Creation."

Our lives bear witness to the dramas concocted by our forebears to create the causeways of a survivable community existence.

All of us *must* perform our parts in the scripts of the Story because we are aware and experience life only as we do so.

The progenitors' Story proscribes and prescribes our conduct and interactions in ways that cause us to do things that are antithetical to our well-being and survival.

We can alter the course and meaning of our lives and the course of cultures and nations in the same way as they were written—with stories.

Agency in life can be achieved by intentionally manipulating the scripts and plots of the Story in ways that make our lives better.

We must stop allowing human history to be conscripted by the progenitors' Story of Life.

We must stop allowing ourselves and our collectives to be seduced and dragged down the plotlines of the progenitors' Story, mindlessly performing fairy tale dramas that seem destined to diminish or destroy us.

Chapter One

Stories Create the Matrix That We Deem Existence, Life and Consciousness of Being

The life that we experience plays out as we commune as individuals in collectives emulating parts in the Story of Life.

The course and meaning of our lives is a Story that was conjured by the progenitors and passed down the generations.

The progenitors' stories orchestrate and bestow purpose, meaning and direction on an erstwhile chaotic unstoried "Universe."

We are conscious of and experience life as we emulate the scripts of the stories of ebbs and flows in the waves of emotions crashing against the granite of consequences that forged a survivable reality.

From birth to death, we dance in choreographed lines and recite scripted speeches of the plots and ploys of the progenitors' Story.

They are the dances that conjure and sculpt our place in creation and opine what it means to Be, and what it is to Be Me within the We.

The ancestors and spirit guides bequeathed to ensuing generations stories that created and refined an increasingly more nuanced, knowable and livable existence, consciousness, reality and Earth.

Their stories scribe the tapestry that is the repository of all knowledge that apprehends, populates, maps, charts and rationalizes the pathways of the meaning of life.

Their Story is the compendium that compasses and harbors every moment from birth to death.

Our existence and consciousness are gentled and stabilized by the Story that is the arc, arch and ark of existence.

The progenitors' Story is the analog for the lives that we live and is preserved as what I call the mind's "Narrative." [1]

---

[1] For a comprehensive discussion of the mind's Narrative, read *On The Nature of Consciousness: The Narrative, a Working Model of Consciousness, the Cognizable, the Known,* by Urrea Jones

The Narrative is the mind's compendium of the stories of the course and meaning of life.

Everything that we know, experience and feel is formulated and bequeathed as an aspect of the Story of Life:

- Where we came from—sample the creation stories of the multiplicity of cultures and civilizations lost to history.
- What the cradle of existence is—peruse the myriad of stories that capture the essence of Mind and Universe.
- Who and what I am—take comfort in stories that bugle the importance of family, the birth of nations and the rise and fall of civilizations, selfhood and individuality.
- Who I share existence with—consider the folklore and fables of the it, he, him, she, her, they, them, we, us, me; and of insiders, outsiders and outliers, gods and goblins, id and ego, ethos and their claims of imprimatur.
- How I am expressed in existence—immerse yourself in paradoxes chronicled as science, psychology, religion, philosophy, sociology, politics, mysticism.
- How my survival is assured—take comfort in the folklore and myths of the bountifulness and harbor of family and collectives.
- Who defends us against the hordes—consider and embrace the orthodoxies spawned in tales of the mythical spirits of tribes, communities, nation-states and the kingdoms of heaven and

hell that shield and defend honor in endless battles between good and evil.

- How to find my way through the valleys of the living—select from among the scripts and chants that illuminate the paths of righteousness and ruin, and of lives lived for good and ill.
- How this all ends—secure safe passage in the books of the dead.
- How it's never over—permit yourself to be unraveled in the teachings of the books of the afterlife and reincarnation.
- What the course and meaning of life is— explore the wisdom of gods, demagogues and gurus chronicled in the teachings of the Bible, Qur'an, Gita, Guru Granth Sahib, Torah, Tripitaka, Perennialism, and the philosophical pathways charted as Existentialism, Constructivism, Pragmatism, Idealism, Positivism, Realism, Romanticism, Progressivism, Humanism.
- How I know I exist—study the stories that declare and anchor our place in the "Cosmos" and community; or just pinch yourself.

All that is life and every aspect of it is understood and lived as stories.

Patterns of sensory inputs trigger apparitions of every kind preserved as reference analogues in the mind's Narrative—our compendium of the stories of the course and meaning of life.

Examples?

Sensory inputs of discrete molecular cocktails and oscillating sound waves carried by the wind are perceived as prophets that portend seduction, fire raging just over the horizon, distant lightning strikes, the whistles of falling bombs, and the bouquet of impending harvests.

Our Narratives are the mind's repository of all the stories known by you and us that are the guides and playbooks of the course and meaning of life cast in every context we imagine.

As strange as it may sound, life is a game of basketball or tennis or chess, writ large.

All human games, including the game of life, are imagined and concocted as stories.

Our lives are expressed as stories.

We live stories that are the blueprints of who we are and our place in the schemes that are inscribed in the Story.

We live stories to explore and traverse our collectives' reality and others' competing realities that we can only imagine because their Narratives are also formulated as stories.

We live stories that build and bind collectives and animate the collective experience.

We tell stories to converse with ourselves and others and to empower and direct action as individuals in collectives.

Emotions are the perfume and spice stories that tether and fuse mind and body, exciting the symbiotic cinematic experience of life.

Everything is a story.

Don't be deceived by the form a story takes. It's still a story.

For example, a map is merely a story etched in analog form on parchment that depicts the lay of the land; so that one can with a glance imagine a route from point "a" to point "b."

We are mesmerized by stories that tame the contours of the emotions of terror, love, freedom, emancipation, gratification, *etc.*

Stories are our inheritance.

Stories are the currency of life.

We are born as stories and live them until we die.

We experience stories that we read as if real, we dream stories as we sleep, we make up stories in order to envision a tomorrow, we tell our children stories to bond with them, we commune by stories, feel by stories, live by stories and die as our stories end.

13

It should come as no surprise that movies, plays, poems and symphonies trigger an experience and surge of emotions with the same fidelity and intensity as those felt on an actual roller coaster ride.

All of existence and the experience of it is projected through the film reel of the Story.

Music, art, math, adventure, landscapes, panoramas, vistas, conquests, tastes, fragrances and mind are just our stories about them.

Stories script and give meaning to life, and captivate, entrance and ensnare us from birth to death.

Life as we know and experience it could not exist without emulating stories about it.

Has this truth evaded you?

Try to perceive, imagine or visualize *anything*, including your experience of being alive, without calling to mind stories that describe its concept, delineate impressions or expressions of it, or that convey its taste, smell, appearance, sounds and the texture of it.

I cannot.

Can you?

All that is knowable and known is tailored and dressed by our stories about it.

There is no existence, consciousness or experience of living without the Story, even if the Cosmos is something more or less than the Story.

Chapter Two

Exposing the Operating Systems and Software of Stories

Agency can be achieved in life if we accept that the "reality" we experience is nothing more than a matrix of stories about the course and meaning of life that are tethered to the Universe and held captive in the mind.

Why is Agency possible when we view life as stories about its course and meaning?

Because if life is stories about it, like any story, the stories about life can be reimagined, abandoned, or new ones written.

Destiny, on the other hand, divine or otherwise, places Agency outside of our reach.

In any case, the structures and strictures of the Story of Life are the mentality that stages life.

Stories trigger a chain reaction that sparks and animates the conscious mind and the experience of living.

Consider that without knowing the preconceived game of chess, we could not play the game of chess.

Likewise, we could not live life as we know it without emulating a preconceived story of the course and meaning of it.

The Story that we emulate was concocted by the progenitors.

Their Story formulates and is the mindscape and landscape that we mine to sustain a survivable reality.

There is no independent reality or life force outside of the Story that imprints an immutable reality and Universe on a mind that is a *tabula rasa* at birth, even if we are a parcel of the "Creation" of "Creators."

The Universe that we are born into informs the mind through the senses of resources that are available to be mined and molded in ways that support our survival, and informs the mind of the perils faced in mining them.

Without the scripts gifted by our forebears, there is no game of life; as there can be no games of basketball, tennis or war without their closed systems of imagined scripts, gambits, courts and venues, players, goals and goalposts, strategies, rules and referees that cue the games.

Stories are the operating systems and software of life.

The operating systems and software that stage and animate the stories that we experience as daily living are closed systems that are the molds of the casts of the experience of life.

Stories appear to require, at minimum, the following factors, coding, programing and characteristics:

- Venues—they postulate the Cosmos, existence, consciousness, mind, self, and fix within them the contours of the ethereal, terrestrial and corporeal; they imagine mathematical and theoretical models and paradigms, art, music, science, fields of wheat, family, tribe, nation-states, stages, canvases, stained glass and symphonies as the panoramas, vistas, tooling and sets of our stories.
- Purpose/Goals/Quests—the original theme of the stories was likely survival, but the themes of the stories can be anything that we dream.
- Plots and Scripts—they imagine and transcribe epic plots and machinations to stage and sustain existence, consciousness and the arc and cycles of lives and civilizations.

- Resources—they posit the stuff of the ethereal and terrestrial that is mined to sustain life.
- Players and Pawns—they dress us as fools and kings, presidents and dictators, rich and poor, high-born and low-born, entitled and disenfranchised, and as civilizations and nations, gods, devils and muses to perform the scripts of the stories.
- Perspectives—they parse the meaning of creation and creator, right and wrong, good and evil, meaningfulness and meaninglessness, fullness and emptiness, thoughtfulness and thoughtlessness, beauty and ugliness, salvation and damnation, demagogues and priests, place and prominence, right-thinking and wrong-thinking, free will and destiny, art and pornography, liberty and justice, life and death, war and peace as ways to congeal and calibrate a meaningful existence.
- Discrete Games and Gambits—they stage war and peace, soccer and football; chart the pathways of triumphs and tragedies, of love and betrayal; wrestle with the implications of being and not; stage us as husbands, wives, families, friends and clans; they chart the routes to enlightenment and eschew ignorance; elevate democracy and denigrate autocracy; praise science and follow mysticism; resist enemies and pursue allies. They compare and contrast musical formulations; they transform religion into philosophy; they seat, crown, sanctify and then replace fathers and chiefs with spirit guides, then gods, then popes, then

kings, then individuality. They obfuscate agency in circular debates about the eminence of fate and free will; and charter the practices of the art of love, hate and indifference. All of the games and gambits are staged to cement commitment to life and community.

To stage reality, our stories seem to require:

- Tools and Tooling—consider the wonders made possible with the tools, structures and gadgets imagined, traced and mapped on blueprints and then sculpted with our hands into things and landscapes. Tools and tooling are the anvils of our stories.
- Repositories—records, statistics and scoresheets preserved in libraries, vaults and memory chips. They preserve the blueprints that are passed to ensuing generations as the templates of the course and meaning of life.
- Goals and Purpose—what's a game for if not for quests, adventures, trials and tragedies?
- Cheers and Cheerleaders—is there a better way to stimulate the games?
- Winners and Losers—triumphs without losers are just not possible.
- Commentary and Commentators—buzz matters.
- Scorekeepers, Referees and Judges—somebody has to make the call.
- Pawns—somebody has to take the fall.
- Enforcers—who can resist a pressed uniform?

- Demagogues—there's nothing quite like a respected narcissist to stink up the works.
- Governance—there's nothing more satisfying than the sting of the whip.
- Hierarchy, Stratification—somebody has to wear the pants and feed on the spoils.
- Acquiescence—just say yes.
- The Choir—is anybody else moved by the preacher? And the congregation says, "Amen."
- Sycophants—resistance is futile.
- Insiders and Outsiders—it's no fun without villains and heroes. Who are you going to blame?
- Leaders and Followers—somebody has to actually fight the battles and those people need to be organized.
- Shared Involvement and Commitment—you're with us or against us. It's just no fun to run with the uninitiated.
- Boundaries Encircling Fields of Play—without membranes, stories dissolve through osmosis.
- Believability—stories must rise to levels that are perceived as real, cognizable and executable or we won't be moved.
- Committed Emotional Involvement—if the stories do not light our fires, we won't play.
- Defensive Structures—it's us or them.
- Efficient Modes of Communication—consider the voices of our stories: language, symbols, digits, pixels, analogues, pictograms, melodies, fragrances, touch, vision, fashion, mathematics, emotions, flags, sculptures.

As in any play, the Story will collapse unless the actors faithfully recite their lines and perform their parts as written, no matter the price or who suffers, even if it is you.

If the Story is not visible to you as what it really is—a fairy tale—you have little chance of recognizing its perfidy and consequences.

And even less chance to resist its seductive power to drag you down plotlines, a restless captive performing the parts, reciting the lines and living the destiny of your character in the Story, whether for ill or good.

Chapter Three

Stories Stage and Animate Existence

Stories are the DNA of life.

Stories ascribe meaning and purpose to existence.

Stories stage, animate and give direction and meaning to life.

Stories sketch, populate and paint the vistas of the dreamscapes and landscapes that we live within.

The Story of Life is the tapestry of the scripts, plots and gambits of a survivable reality that was conjured by the progenitors.

You, I, and we experience living as we emulate parts in the scripts of the Story.

The progenitors' stories conjured creation, existence, reality, purpose, family, clan, tribe, nation, civilization, birth and death, and everything else that is known and knowable to us.

The lives that we experience are as players in ensembles emulating the vignettes of the Story of Life in its vistas of imagined mindscapes and landscapes.

All players and ensembles must know and perform their parts as written in the Story, whether for good or ill.

In the schemes that are our daily lives, every place and part is scripted, and every action and reaction accounted for.

The same is true for all of our novels, computer programs, games, plays, paintings, sculptures, cartoons, symphonies, ideas, ideations, landscapes, vistas, constellations and epochs.

All players must acquiesce in their places and parts as written in the Story and each must speak and perform their parts faithfully.

Otherwise, there is no coherent story to live, only chaos.

Consider why.

A football game will disintegrate if players refuse to follow the rules and playbooks.

You can't play tennis and basketball at the same time. The game has to be staged as one or the other.

The same is true of all stories, including the Story that we are living.

Our parts and prerogatives in the plots and ploys are invariably circumscribed by our "markers."

The "avatars" that bear our markers and are our characters in the game of life are assigned by the accident of birth, not merit or fairness.

Markers are the sum of the stories about a person that delineate who and what they are, and fix their social status, place, prerogatives, and access to resources in the schemes and scheming of collectives.

Examples: entitlement to land or throne as a birthright, social class as a basis for access to resources, union membership as a job requirement, Christianity as the Gatekeeper to Heaven.

All the characters in ensembles have to share the same scripts, follow the same plots, perform in the same venues and acquiesce in assigned roles and parts in the scripts of the Story—whether as master or slave, parent or child, preacher or parishioner, Othello or Desdemona, prince or pauper, predator or prey—or the Story will collapse.

Maturation is the process of internalizing the scripts, storylines and vignettes of the Story of Life.

As in the performance of any play, we must memorize the scripts so that we can perform them.

The Story is like a game of basketball or tennis, writ large.

Your character in the Story of Life is the equivalent of a guard in the game of basketball.

To perform the Story, we must learn our roles in the Story's plots, learn which parts we can be cast in, and also learn all other players' parts in the enterprise.

The parts that we emulate in the Story are circumscribed by our markers' characteristics, e.g., gender, ethnicity, social status, religion, appearance and membership in families, clans, tribes and nations that control access to resources; and little else.

The Story can unravel or collapse if players don't acquiesce in their intertwined and reciprocal places and parts in the storyline.

We all know the scripts of our collectives' Story.

Moreover, there is little variation within and between the themes of collectives, except that "the others" are always labeled and cast as villains and interlopers.

The plots, players and parts of the Story are the tapestry of life.

To step out of character, place or the script is to step out of existence.

The story format is the mental formulation that builds the fortresses and scripts of life and the themes that animate them.

A story is the instructions, recipe, coding and programming that serves as reference, roadmap and guide in administering, organizing, capturing and allocating resources to achieve some purpose, goal, state, ideation or ideal.

Our stories do not reflect an immutable systemic reality that is ordained by the Cosmos; rather they capture and stage the gauntlets and gambits that have been crafted by generations over millennia in the quest to survive and then thrive.

The Story is the fairy tale that conjured a survivable and meaningful reality and structured the chaos that was encountered upon crawling out of the abyss into the landscapes and dreamscapes that the progenitors imagined, and we now inhabit.

Our human reality is purpose-built and exists and is staged at the convergence of mind and body as the body informs the mind and the mind directs the body.

The will to survive spawned the story equation that creates workable and shareable mechanisms to exploit resources to support survival.

All that is the human experience is concocted and captured in the Story.

The story equation formulates the instructions to organize resources in the pursuit of goals, states, ideas and ideations.

Stories are the blueprints that inscribe the directions to construct our reality and everything in it.

Our stories anchor generation after generation in the foundation that is necessary to support successive communities in an endless quest for a meaningful life.

The stories contain the instructions for exploiting and manipulating resources, including each other, to achieve collective goals, ideations and more refined states.

They preserve and recite the steps and sequences that organize information and factors necessary to build and sustain community.

The story formulation can be expressed in any format, including language, map, picture, chart, sculpture, scripture, symphony, collective, institution and individual.

The Story creates and anchors the reality that we live, live in and share with each other.

Every aspect of the Story is scripted.

For the community to survive, players must slavishly follow the scripts that create and sustain its existence.

Agency can only be grasped through a mentality that posits everything as story, not destiny or fate.

If we can accept that the Story is just a fairy tale, life can be lived as an exploration rather than a tangle of fate.

Chapter Four

It's the Scripts and Plots of the Story That Overwhelm You, It's Not Your Fault

As in every story or play, the symphony that is the Story of Life only resonates if the characters in the enterprise (our avatars) faithfully strum the notes and chords as scored.

Our avatars (corpora) are the characters that perform our parts in the Story.

I submit that the caricatures that are the vessels of our minds must be avatars.

I know that the essence of my being is something much more than my corpus. And so do you.

By the way, we don't get to choose our avatars.

Our souls are fused with avatars at birth. We have no say in it.

Surely, there can be no failure or fault where there is no say.

The Story must be a closed system. The same is true of all stories.

Everything needed to tell the story has to be included in its script, painting, fresco, fable, parable, hypothesis, formula, thesis, ...

As players, we can add depth and nuance to our characters' performances, but if players alter their performances in ways that impede the development of the plotline of the script, the plot may collapse—depending on the player's relative importance to the plot.

All story formats, like motion pictures, plays and paintings, will fail to convey the intended message, metaphor or parable, or fail to resonate, if their scripts are not written as closed systems, i.e., all of the stuff necessary to develop the themes and allegories of the story must be included in the story's script.

Each player's roles, parts and speeches in the Story chart that player's destiny, even though players have little say in what their character must say and do to support the storyline.

In every performance, all characters must mostly ape and speak their parts as written and stomach the sting of their performances.

Whether hero or victim, prince or pauper, master or slave, or all of them at once, the parts and speeches as written are a player's fate.

There are at least two compelling, interrelated reasons why players are conscripted and circumscribed by their avatars:

> First, for any story to be told, it has to chart and chronicle the plights and fates of all players and ensembles in the fixed constellation of the plots and ploys penned by the playwright. All players *must* faithfully perform their parts as written or the story will collapse.

> Second, the Story of Life *is* life—i.e., the life that we live and the reality that it portends is our existence. If players do not acquiesce in the stories' schemes and plots, and faithfully perform the intertwined parts and traverse the pathways as they are written in the Story, reality will fracture, become chaotic or collapse.

We exist and are conscious as we emulate intermeshed parts and recite inextricably tangled speeches in the Story that scripts the pathways and meaning of life.

If the stories collapse, reality itself collapses and *we cease to exist in part, or whole.*

To exist and feel relevant in the Story, we must be faithful to our characters, even when unpalatable.

Reviews of our performances are unavoidable.

The most caustic reviews are our own.

The reviews are not about personal deficiencies, inadequacies, faults or failures, innocence or guilt, or personal at all.

They are critiques of the performances of the characters that we are forced to play in the scripts of the Story to experience our daily lives.

Although they feel deeply personal, they are not critiques of us.

At stake in every speech, for every player, in every play, is not whether *"to be or not to be"* as Shakespeare's Hamlet mused; but rather, whether to submit to ordained parts in the Story of Life or ***be not***.

In our daily living we feel it as we become invisible, unseen, misunderstood, disrespected, devalued, unappreciated, ignored or irrelevant to those around us.

We feel it as we lose our audience mid-speech or lose command of the stage. The loss smarts as we become unseen.

But it is important to remember that the Story was conjured to create a stable and survivable *community reality*, not a survivable reality for individuals who quickly expire in the crucible of life.

Our parts in the Story were written primarily to sustain the ark of community, not the individual.

Even so, the community is the womb and harbor of our finite existence.

It is our island in a sea of chaos.

All must play their parts in ensembles as scripted to sustain the community that gives our short lives context and meaning.

Millennia is the arc of the Story. Our parts in it are measured in decades.

The survival of collectives, not individuals, is the primary thesis of the Story of Life.

Even so, the Story *is* the Story of the community that cradles each of us.

Consider the Faustian bargain made in exchange for community:

- We must acquiesce in scripts that circumscribe the pathways to a meaningful and fulfilling personal life; scripts that set expectations for our place, prominence and access in collectives; and that prescribe and proscribe how our lives can be lived.
- We must acquiesce in stories that impose standards and expectations of every kind on everything about us—how we should look, how we should feel, the acceptable pathways to a meaningful and fulfilling life, what permissible behavior is and is not, what acceptable conduct is and is not, what family is and what family feels like, what friendship is and who we can fraternize with—all of the strictures overripe figs fostering festering feelings of disappointment and guilt.
- We are corseted by our avatars' markers that circumscribe our access in collectives. In our journeys through life, we experience profound and devastating disappointment as we realize that life's not going like it's supposed to for us. We all feel deep down that our fate is our fault (but it's not). So, we target others as interlopers and bogeymen so that they, not we, take the fall. No better way than a purported conspiracy of others to numb the conscience; and, as added bonuses, conspiracies are impervious to evidence and reason and feed the fires of outrage.

- Our access to the resources of life is largely dependent on whether our avatar is deemed "right" for a part in the community. If not, we cannot be cast in the part. In short, our characters' markers determine what parts we get to play, who and what we are, our place, prominence and access in the dramas and, sadly, how we feel about ourselves. It's not that we're male or female, black or white, Christian or Jew that determines our access and self-esteem. It's the positive and negative imprimaturs that are associated with our avatars that determine the role we are permitted to play in the Story and what we and others think of ourselves. Imprimaturs are the measure of our worth and self-esteem.

- Our avatars' markers include belief systems, appearance, temperament, gait, speech, behavior, scent, morality, mannerisms, gender, skin tone, relationships, propensities, conduct, position, education, status, and all other factors that prescribe and proscribe a person's character, characteristics and their place and prominence in collectives.

- Our characters' markers are the principal determinants of social access, status and prominence.

- Our characters' markers are the primary determinants of how we are perceived by ourselves and others.

- We are bound to follow the scripts written for our characters no matter the personal costs.

- Our emotions are the acid that keep us on script.
- We have to endure reviews of the performance of our avatars. Though painful, the reviews, whether ours or others', are simply scoring our characters' performances, and nothing more.
- Our parts in the Story are our destiny.
- Our parts in the Story are our existence and are what tethers us to community.
- We have no existence outside of the plots and gambits of the Story.
- If we fail to play our characters convincingly and as written, or stray from their pathways, we become antithetical to the Story and are sanctioned or ignored by the other players in our ensembles.
- We must mostly ape our parts no matter how we feel about them, including the nasty and repugnant aspects of them.
- It's not principle, fault or failure that have us on a leash in the Story. It's that we cease to exist if we don't perform our parts in the Story as they are scripted.
- We have to know all the parts and plots of the Story to participate; but we only get to play the parts scripted for our avatar based on hierarchical structures demarcated by race, gender, orientation, status, politics, country, family, clan, tribe, education; we are denied the parts that our characters are not allowed to play.
- Conflict inevitably occurs within and between tribes as each casts the other as interloper in the

competition for scarce resources in the progenitors' zero-sum reality Story.

- Conflict inevitably occurs between us as we each lay claim to the places of preeminence in our tribes; the places that determine who gets to eat first at the harvest or hunt.
- We are compelled to emulate the same failed plots over and over again because they are the fates written for our characters.
- Master and servant, pawn and king are all captives of the Story.

The Story is able to overwhelm us and drag us down rabbit holes because, whether prince or pawn, African or Asian, educated or ignorant, married or single, male or female, you will cease to exist if you don't faithfully emulate your part in the Story.

Which means you have no choice.

Either we recite our scripted lines and play our scripted parts in the Story, even as they sully our souls, or we cease to exist.

It is nonsense to speak of fault or responsibility absent an understanding that your existence, no matter how emotionally charged, is just the delusion of a fairy tale.

It is meaningless emotional melodrama to claim responsibility, failure or fault as scripted players, emulating roles in scripted gambits, in the conjured constellations of painful plots and ploys that are not of our making.

These emotions are the arrogant illusory indulgences of the ignorant.

You cannot claim fault or responsibility unless, knowing your predicament, you persist in the folly of your character.

Chapter Five

Story, the Mentality of Agency

Stories!

Why can't I Be without Thee?

Because without myths, there are no scripts, places or reasons for You to Be.

Without the Story, there is no place to be born, live and die; no people or games to play, and no trinkets to adorn us for the minuets that are the dances of life.

The story format itself triggers our experience of any "reality," whether the vignette performed is "real" or "imagined."

Let me demonstrate what I mean when I say that you cannot experience anything without knowing stories about it.

A few hopefully entertaining examples:

- You cannot dress fashionably for the scene unless you shop knowing the homies' "must haves" for the fashionable wardrobe.
- You cannot be the consummate lover unless you have the scripts and scoresheet of the lover in your head as you do the "dirty deed."
- You cannot steal your neighbor's spouse unless you've mastered the scripts of the artistry and the tango of the Casanova.
- You cannot say mass unless you know the litany.
- You cannot be a good parent unless you've learned scripts of good parenting as a child or by reading the right books.
- You cannot get from here to there unless you have a map in head or hand and an intent to do so; or do you prefer dead reckoning?
- You cannot experience betrayal without a roadmap and its attendant emotional jingles pounding in your head. Soaps are a helpful reference.
- All of us know that you can't judge a book by its cover.

Sorry to dispel delusions of creativity, spontaneity and of roads untraveled. Predictably, even the road untraveled has pathways.

For committed delusionists, your best shots are to improvise or go for nuance. But even these require scripts to ape in the performance of them.

In your entire life journey, there are no roads without maps and no uncharted domains to explore, even though we are certain that there are.

The heavy lifts—creating and scripting the stories of the course and meaning of community life—were made by our progenitors and spirit guides over millennia in the epochs of lost cultures and civilizations.

Our lives are experienced as we emulate parts in the plots and ploys of the progenitors' Story—many of them are the same coats in different colors.

The scripts that we live are manifestations of the dreamscapes and landscapes that were conjured to stage the plots and ploys of the farce that we channel as life.

All of it is make-believe, *except* the consequences.

The story format itself triggers our experience of anything as "reality," whether the experience is "real" or "imaginary."

Bear witness with me to the progenitors' revelations in their soliloquies.

"The truth is that when our consciousness emerged from the abyss, the smells, feels, sounds and sights of the nameless, meaningless place we found ourselves in were intoxicating.

"We were snared by this place and suspended in the grip of its intoxication.

"I vowed to do anything to remain in this wondrous swirl of sensations.

"Those of us who did not take the vow slipped back into the abyss.

"I was aware that I was alone and lost, and that the things that I was trying to swallow were trying to swallow me.

"We craved the warmth of closeness, but we were as lost to each other as we were to everything around us.

"We were untethered, and without meaning or understanding.

"None of us could comprehend what was happening around us or why; or knew a way to tame it.

"But somehow, I understood that I could not remain in this place, unless together we named the spaces and places and things within it, and together dreamed ways to appropriate all of it for ourselves.

"Maybe it was whispered to us by the spirits that created us.

"We had to map this place so that we could find sustenance, track down company for warmth and find and dwell in its pleasure places.

"You know what we came up with, don't you?

"You don't?

"Is it because you believe all of it was created and given to us by forces and spirits that are greater than our imaginations?

"We did it by concocting stories about everything in this place, and so we did.

"Our stories gave this place form, substance, meaning and life.

"Reality is composed in the stories that we dreamed and then chiseled with our hands and explored with our sight, hearing, smell and touch.

"By making up stories about us and the place we were in, we staked a claim to existence and then mined it.

"Intoxication surrendered to imagination.

"We conjured stories that painted the vistas of the landscapes and dreamscapes of mind and body and that charted pathways that gave life meaning.

"We named the places and things revealed to us in the roars and whispers of the spirits that inhabit them to fashion a reality that placed the earth under foot so that we could walk upright on solid ground and hunt.

"We named the apparitions that we hunted by the sounds they made, the speed of their flight, their musk in the wind and the outline of their shadows.

"As we named them, the apparitions were revealed to our eyes.

"We shared their names with each other and traced their likeness on sandstone and cave walls with our blood so that we all could know what to hunt.

"As we hunted and foraged, we formulated the spaces where prey hid and places that sustenance flowered by the contours revealed to us by the spirits of the hills and valleys of the place we were in.

"The spirits gave us seers who could wield fire with their bare hands.

"We hummed then gave words to melodies that celebrated how we and the place we found ourselves came to be, and of the creators that fashioned us and all the things in this place.

"All of it revealed in chanting incantations given to us by the spirits of creation.

"We knew that the Creators couldn't be one of us.

"We see where we come from and know where our bodies go when our spirits release them.

"We drop from our mothers' bodies nine full moons after they surrender in the embrace of our fathers.

"Our bodies rot and return to the earth as dust and our spirits fall back into the abyss when we die.

"We showed our submission to the will of the Creators by making sacrifices to them, so that they will not strike us down.

"Some of us saw that those who hunted as one had more to eat than those who did not.

"They ran down more prey, took more from others, and captured the most givers of pleasure.

"We named them 'the many as one.'

"So, we dreamed and told stories of unification so that we could also hunt as one.

"They are the stories of the union of man, woman and child to bind us as brothers and sisters in kinships.

"They are the stories of tribe and clan that bind us as communities.

"We dreamed stories to name and fix all of the things in our landscapes and dreamscapes and that tether each to the other.

"Without the stories we could not build and tame the bounty of the place where we found ourselves.

"We weaved stories that fused us together so that we could act as one against the forces of death.

"You know these stories as the things that we wield to mold and direct us in the ways we harness the forces and power of community.

"You know their names, plots and scripts.

"We passed them from generation to generation in art, edifices, sculptures, folklore, myths, texts, plays, poems, stained glass windows, cinema, architecture, monuments, cemeteries, cathedrals, mathematics, languages, libraries, mausoleums, ruins, hypotheses, philosophies, religions, civilizations.

"You also know all the players and props in the stories:

> "Male and female, mother and father, kinship and kind, clan and tribe, state and nation-state, empire and colony.

> "Insider and outsider, prince and pauper, barbarian and crusader, devil and angel.

"Creator, father, spirit guide, shaman, chief, rabbi, Imam, teacher, philosopher, psychologist, sociologist, king, emperor, president, oligarch, czar, demagogue, trendsetter, early adopter, self.

"Church, state, colony, military-industrial complex, international cartel, world economy.

"Spirits, mystics, metaphysicians, scientists, popes, potentates, demagogues, social psychologists, behavioral economists.

"Place, prominence, gender, race, status, body-image.

"Matriarchy, county, monarchy, dictatorship, republic, parliamentary democracy, representative democracy, oligarchy.

"To feel alive, we chanted and performed the dramas forced upon us by the creators, even though we were hapless pawns in their dramas, numbed by the battle to eat or be eaten in the quagmire of good and evil.

"We were just pawns for the amusement of the Creators.

"We were compelled to choose when we had no choice.

"So, we imagined ways to deceive the gods, and then set about to displace them.

"That is why over the spans of generations our cults of spirit guides submitted to cults of shaman, chiefs, prophets, judges, saviors and philosophers; that gave way to demagogues, popes and potentates who bowed down to the armies of pharaohs, kings, czars, emperors and states, and, at long last, the cult of the individual—all of them taking on the mantles of god or demon.

"All of it to no avail.

"All of it self-deception.

"We persisted in believing that our Story was the 'revealed,' rather than a reality that we conjured.

"The Story that we created to anchor existence, consciousness and community threatens to destroy our existence.

"The burden and pain that we endure as we play our parts and speak our lines in the Story have become overwhelming.

"Disappointment is the residue of the scripts and plots in beguiling tales that drag us, emptied of feeling, down the pathways of the *proper* course and meaning of life.

"All of the exhausting plotting and machinations; the ruthless appropriation of resources and the justifications for doing so; the tragedy and betrayal; the endless crusades and massacres, wars and rumors of wars; the disappointed expectations and the poisoning of the connections that harbor us; the destruction of the place where we live.

"All of it to appropriate and hoard in a zero-sum quagmire.

"All of it too much to shoulder.

"Too many of us are not able to cope in our parts in the scripts and with the treachery that is woven into the Story.

"People are unhappy with themselves and each other, and the disappointment spawned by expectations that are idealized in the templates of a meaningful life that is always beyond our reach.

"There is no solace in the promise of a more perfect union in the afterworld or in a second, third, fourth, fifth chance to hit the jackpot in the next incarnation.

"None of our tales calm our spirits or modulate our treatment of ourselves and each other.

"The Story is a powerful tool for capturing and appropriating resources in the erstwhile game of survival.

"Yet, the Story fails to quiet the critical and destructive chatter in our heads; fails to make us truly happy and unafraid; fails to make us treat others with the respect and deference that we demand for ourselves; and fails to answer for our existence.

"Worse still, it causes us to prey on ourselves and each other with impunity, deplete the earth's bounty, and poison the earth with the plastics of our imaginations.

"The Story is collapsing and us with it.

"It's time to abandon the Story that was spawned in the quicksand of the zero-sum conundrum and is the license to do anything to survive, no matter the cost."

Chapter Six

Claiming Agency in Life by Seizing the Redemptive Power of Story

If, as I posit, the Story is the mentality, i.e., the mental paradigm or device, that creates and stages the experience of living, *then*, we can seize Agency in life by challenging the themes and assumptions of the Story and by tweaking our parts and roles in it.

You'll forgive my penchant for compound sentences. It's my fault, not yours, if you have to pause to unravel, consider and embrace their meaning and significance.

The Story that we emulate was not written by us.

The Story was hewed by the progenitors in their struggle to populate the survivable reality, which has been passed to us through the generations.

The progenitors' Story is our inheritance.

The progenitors, not we, charted and paved the causeways of life.

Their Story creates and is the master of our fate.

The progenitors' conjurings formed and fixed the themes and pathways of life, and our parts and places in the dreamscapes and landscapes of imagined scripts that now chart our destiny.

That destiny can be altered if we seize Agency and reimagine the Story, rather than submit ourselves to being swept away, bobbing in the currents and eddies of ancient scripts and texts.

Face It, You're Living a Fairy Tale

In the search for the keys to Agency, it seems to me that we must accept that the Story is the Pied Piper of life.

How?

Because the Story *is* reality and our experience of it.

I intend no disrespect for our presumed importance in the Cosmos, but we really should expose the Pied Piper's trickery.

Let's begin by talking about how plays are imagined and written.

Permit me the latitude of simplicity to illustrate.

All plays, including the Story that we are emulating, require themes, players, ensembles, venues, plots and gambits.

Isn't this how all stories are incubated?

In the metamorphous from the imagined to the penned, the playwright sketches a storyboard or scribes a synopsis of plots, characters, and the major themes of the play, book, commercial, cartoon or movie.

She then tailors and dresses the poem, novel, symphony or screenplay by weaving the themes, melodies, plots, ploys and the interactions of players in the venues of the storyline into a "statement" about something.

All is revealed in the speeches and actions of characters and ensembles.

For a story to resonate, every composition is crafted to faithfully portray the themes, plots and machinations of all manner of ballerinas twirling in a multiplicity of vignettes that are woven into the tapestry of the story.

Let me illustrate how we are characters emulating parts in scripts that stage the life that we live.

Consider the family.

The players: parent(s) and child(ren).

The plot: loving parent(s) providing a "nurturing home" in which the child(ren) learns the skills (spiels) needed to survive and flourish as part of the community.

You know the varied themes and takes on family life.

The evidence?

All of us have little trouble describing in minute detail the many ways family stories play out and the plots, ploys and derivations of family life. We couldn't perform parts in the ensemble if we did not know all of the parts in the enterprise.

Isn't family members' failure to play their parts like they're supposed to at the root of family dysfunction?

The empirical proof?

Take a moment to picture in your mind a few family vignettes.

Describe scenarios depicting some of the more prominent themes of family life, like nurturing parents, understanding parents, family triumphs and tragedies, family outings, good parents, bad parents, good parenting, bad parenting, good homes, happy homes, unhappy families, kids to be proud of, attractive kids, happy kids.

On reflection, you will find that you have well-developed templates in your mind of the families that we are born into and forced to endure.

Moreover, we judge the quality of our family experience by reference to these templates.

Further evidence?

Compare notes of family ideations with members of your family, friends and acquaintances.

You'll discover that they too articulate well-developed notions of family that are the same or similar in theme and scope as yours, even if distinguishable in detail.

We all know and share remarkably similar stories about every aspect of our lives.

How else could we live as communities?

Let me suggest a few more examples.

Compare your concepts of the following with those of others and see whether we all are mostly on the same pages, of the same plots, of the same scripts, of the same Story of the pathways of life:

- What it feels like to be in love and loved.
- What it means to be alive.
- What it means to be a good citizen.
- What it means to be a good friend.
- Whether it's better to be rich or poor.
- What makes us feel safe.
- What the characteristics of a valued friend are.
- What makes someone a traitor.
- What life without purpose feels like.
- Whether there is life after death.
- What democracy, autocracy, oligarchy are.
- What the difference between a house and a home is.
- What a solar system is.
- What the difference between war and peace is.
- What a spouse is.
- What a mouse is.

All of us know and apprehend the Story that creates and charts our shared experience of the course and meaning of life and our parts in it.

The Story is the bedrock of community.

Without shared scripts, plots and parts in the Story, even the antithetical ones, there can be no community in which to live and thrive.

You Can Demonstrate to Yourself That
We Are Emulating Parts in a Myth

I hope I'm not belaboring the evidence thing, but consider the multitude and multiplicity of self-verifiable empirical evidence that suggests that we are characters emulating parts in the Story.

It seems to me that nothing we do could be choreographed as a line dance, or dance of any kind, if the dancers didn't know the melodies and the body movements that express the dance.

Again, compare notes with family and friends to see whether you share similar ideations:

- An understanding of who we are, what we can become, and where we fit in the scheme of things vis-à-vis others.
- An understanding of our respective place, prominence and access to collectives' territories and resources vis-à-vis others.
- An understanding of our social spaces, roles and prerogatives vis-à-vis others.

We also share perspectives.

Consider the following:

- Our tribes and collectives speak the same tongue.
- One language is translatable into another.
- We all are conscious in the same present.

- We pursue standard models of the Universe.
- We attempt to standardize everything.
- Our kin and clan share common friends and enemies.
- We act as one in mobs.
- We all chase similar dreams.
- We all group together for defense.
- Our groups can act as one.
- We erect similar edifices, barriers and cathedrals.
- We build alliances against each other.
- Our tribe's worship is the true worship.
- We are all compelled by the same zero-sum paradox as the reason to hoard.
- We all have expectations and disappointments fueled by group norms.
- We all aspire and fall short.
- We all feel the whiplash of triumph and tragedy.
- We are all driven and swept away by hormones and emotions.
- We all hear whispers in our heads.
- We all make mistakes.
- We all repeat mistakes.
- We all are born and die.
- We all are haunted by failure.
- We all have a past, a present and the promise of a future.
- We all fail to learn from the past.
- We all have memories.
- We all seek sanctuary, whether family, gang, clan, tribe, country or culture.

- We all mount quests, adventures and crusades.
- We all calculate right and wrong.
- We all yearn for something more.
- We all go along to get along.
- We all are deceitful.
- We all play field and board games.

Consider that we all seek to answer similar questions about life:

- Why are we here?
- What does it mean to be happy?
- Why do we yearn for the company of family and friends?
- What makes us happy or unhappy?
- What is justice?
- Why am I misunderstood and unappreciated?
- What is my purpose in life?
- What threatens our safety and wellbeing?
- Why are we stressing?
- What is a successful life?
- What is tyranny?
- What is important in life?
- What kind of person do I want to be?
- Does anyone know how I really feel and who I really am?
- What are my weaknesses?
- What are my strengths?
- Why do I feel alone?
- Why are we so afraid?

We could not live as communities without a shared Story that choreographs and coordinates our interactions with each other.

Without the Story, there can be no community.

It's Not About Fault

No matter how emotionally charged or high-minded our feelings are about responsibility and guilt, it is futile to assume fault or responsibility if we are unwitting characters in somebody else's fairy tale.

Responsibility and fault are meaningless emotional hyperbole if we are the hapless prisoners of scripted plots and gambits and are emulating ordained parts in a Story that is not of our making.

The Story that we emulate was conjured by the progenitors, not us.

No one can be at fault unless after realizing their plight they persist in aping their characters' parts in the Story, whether for good or ill.

Feelings of fault are useless illusory indulgences, unless we continue the blameworthy conduct knowing our plight.

Moreover, even if we know the stories that promise the good life or life well lived, there cannot be individual responsibility or fault in the failure to realize them if we don't also know the stories that map the pathways to the promised lands.

Stories drive the course and meaning of life, even if they are fairy tales.

Red Alert, the Signposts to Agency

I have no doubt that you are familiar with the seductive power of storytelling to drag you down plotlines, tingling from the thrill of the ride.

Consider the lure of the intrigue of an Agatha Christie novel, the comfort taken in the musings of a good jazz soloist, the chilling horror of going down with the Titanic in high definition and Dolby surround sound.

The experience of these tales is visceral.

Doesn't matter that none of them are really happening.

You experience dread as screeching violins announce an impending shark attack in *Jaws*.

You brace yourself in panic against your cinema seat as the roller coaster on the screen crests, then pauses, then makes the inexorable plunge.

Makes no difference that you are not on that roller coaster.

Pride wells in your chest as the national anthem plays.

You're moved to tears by harrowing accounts of the suffering of others.

You feel the force as you bear witness to the struggle between good and evil chronicled in *Star Wars*.

You feel aroused by the fragrance of a lover's perfume, even when they are not there.

You are overtaken by rage even as you are entranced by news footage of war atrocities.

You join in the dance of the performers while planted in your seat as you are dazzled at the ballet.

None of it is real.

All of it is experienced as real, even though you know it's not.

All of it visceral illusions triggered by the magical power of stories to override reason.

The Story that we emulate has the same power to viscerally drag us down its storyline as does the roller coaster flickering on the silver screen.

Your being is helpless to resist the power of the Story to move mind and body.

The Story, like all tales, has the power to force us to feel and do things that we would resist if we saw it for what it really is, a fairy tale.

We are spellbound by the Pied Piper of the Story.

Let me posit a few everyday situations that should sound the alarm that we are prisoners of the Story of Life:

- We go along to get along—just trying to fit in, are you? At what cost?
- We find ourselves in arguments and have no idea what we are arguing about or why— 'cause it's the principle of the thing?
- We say things to each other that we don't really mean—'cause you feel cornered? Or is it that you believe it is your *moral duty* to force the other guy to toe the line?
- We find ourselves criticizing others for doing exactly the same things that we do—what's good for the goose *isn't* good for the gander? How can that be?
- We are mostly unhappy with ourselves—you just aren't the person that you are supposed to be or expected to be? By whose standards? Who sets the standards? Was it you? The body you're trapped in doesn't pass muster. Like you chose it or something?
- Voices in our heads hound us—you haven't noticed that the criticisms are almost always offered when it's too late to do anything about it, rarely before? Worse, you're being chastised

for failings over which you have little or no control.

- We don't like who and what we are—that doesn't make much sense since the skin we're in is an accident of birth.
- We're only being vindictive to teach the other guy a lesson—standards must be maintained at all costs.
- We're denigrative and dismissive of each other—clearly, I'm right and you're not.
- We are justified in exploiting outsiders— what's the problem? After all, they are not like us, and they are trying to displace us, anyway. "We will not be displaced."
- We're always looking for the advantage—give me a break. It's a dog-eat-dog world.
- We allow others to put us in "our place"—face it, some of us are better than others.
- We are burdened by self-criticism—I'm just not good enough.
- You're into the blame game—it wasn't me. The devil made me do it. I had no choice. They wouldn't let me.
- Everything is a conspiracy—"We will not be replaced."
- We ignore anything that contradicts our orthodoxy—don't bother me with facts.
- We make the same mistakes and miscalculations over and over again—isn't that the same loser as last time?
- You keep doing things that you don't want to do—that's what happens when scripts are your destiny.

- Your behavior in situations surprises even you—that's just not possible is it, unless ... you're not in charge.
- Déjà vu.

Stories are the mentality that create the experience of being alive. We are the prisoners of their scripts.

Stories are the Pied Piper of life.

We experience life as the Story drags us down its plotlines, whether for good or ill.

Seizing the Levers of Agency to Make Life Better

As I have already proposed, if life is just the Story about it, it seems to me that we can seize Agency in our lives by challenging the themes and assumptions of the Story and by tweaking our roles in it as we perform our bits in the dreamscapes and landscapes of the Story.

Agency, at minimum, requires a seat at the table and a voice in the enterprise.

Each of us exists as an avatar that encapsulates determinants that proscribe, prescribe and circumscribe our social status, place, prominence and, most importantly, access to collective resources.

Our avatars stain our corpora.

The character that plays you in life delineates and telegraphs your access, place, prominence, position and social status for all to see.

You do not get to choose your avatar.

Our avatars are an accident of birth.

Factors like gender, race, ethnicity, family, kinship, tribe and religion are some of the markers of your character.

Our markers are the major factor that determines the way we live and experience our lives.

Our avatars' markers in large part determine our self-image, self-esteem, social place, prerogatives, entitlements, and the roles and parts that we are eligible to play in the Story of Life.

Consider for a moment the social roles, whether quarterback, president or plumber, that are or have been outside of the reach of females, Catholics, Irishmen and members of lower castes because of their markers.

In terms of the lives we live, we cannot find fulfillment in the good life, the happily-ever-after life, or the pie-in-the-sky life if access to them is blocked because of the markers of our avatars.

* * *

Before we move on in our discussion of ways to seize the levers of Agency, it would seem helpful to get our bearings within the structures of the "Narrative" that I posit is the mind's repository of the Story of Life.

Don't lose sight of the proposition that the progenitors' Story creates the reality, i.e., the scripts of the drama that we live and experience as life.

The Story that was concocted by the progenitors creates, stabilizes and anchors our very existence.

Without the Story, our reality and the experience of it would not exist.

You are a character emulating a part in the Story of Life that was conceived by the progenitors.

Their Story is no different than our preconceived games of football, checkers or monopoly.

Games cannot be played until they are conceived and coalesce as a discrete enterprise.

The Story that we emulate was conceived over millennia by the progenitors and is imprinted in our minds as our Narrative.

As I indicated earlier, the Narrative is the mind's repository of the compendium of the Story of Life.

The Narrative is the templates, scripts and transcripts of the drama that each of us performs as life.

Our lives emulate the progenitors' Story of Life.

Our lives emulate their fairy tale.

Putting aside the intervention of the "forces of nature," the major players in the mental tapestry of the Story that stages life are: the self, the other-selves and our collectives.

A passage taken from *On the Nature of Consciousness* illustrates the role of the major players:

"The story of the self that is inscribed in the [mind's] self-narrative is the *marker* and *placeholder* that identifies, describes, and distinguishes the self for the self and from other selves. The marker-placeholder encapsulates belief systems, temperament, gait, speech, behavior, appearance, scent, moral systems, mannerisms, gender, race, relationships, propensities, conduct, position, education, status, and all other factors that are the markers of a person's character, characteristics, place, and prominence. It encapsulates and distinguishes the self from others to the self and to others. It telegraphs determinatives of access, place, prominence, social status, and position. It establishes pecking order and social stratification.

It defines and pegs the individual's place, prominence, entitlement, privilege, and role in society. The importance of a person's marker and place may explain the obsession with status, reputation, face, loss of face, *etc.* Even though the self-narrative is the marker-placeholder, *it is not the essence or soul.*

"The [mind's] other-selves-narratives operate in the same manner as the self-narrative. Other-selves-narratives allow the self to conceptualize, calculate, act, and interact based on social place, prominence and the status of others and extend due deference—even if the assessment is woefully inaccurate. People struggle to control others' image of themselves and to force others' compliance to their self-image by signaling their place and prominence via mannerisms, affect, dress, job, estate, ancestry, prowess, even if they are just passing.

"The [mind's] collectives-narratives are the administrative functionary of goals, aspirations, and the policing of organized activity in collectives. The collectives-narratives impose order, standards, expectations, and concerted activity. They are the administrators of command and control. The collectives-narratives are the storybooks and playbooks of organizational structures, individual and collective actions, the allocation, and distribution of resources. The collectives-narratives do not portend potential or creativity, they reflect the present social matrix and stratification.

"The Narrative is the scaffolding, the storybook and meaning of life clad in substance and forged over mindless millennia. It captures and inscribes in the brain the replete analogues of everything.

"The Narrative [the mind's repository of the compendium of the stories of life] *is not destiny*; *it is the existential.*

"The Narrative *is not fate or the master of fate*, except when left untended by *the will.*

"The Narrative *is not the playwright, it illuminates and stages life's venue.*

"The self-narrative *is not the essence or soul, it is the self's marker-placeholder, lane.*"[2]

I also need to call out the voices in our heads.

A passage taken from *Without Stories, There is No Universe, Existence, Reality or You*[3] serves well here:

"I'm going to take a few paragraphs to talk about those voices in your head that are

---

[2] *On the Nature of Consciousness*, at pages 39 through 41.
[3] *Without Stories, There is No Universe, Existence, Reality or You*, by Urrea Jones.

sometime distracting, sometime pesky, sometime irritating, sometime *really* irritating, sometime the cause of sleepless nights, and for some overwhelming.

"The lucky among us find the voices uplifting and supportive, but this is rarely the case.

"Who are those voices?

"They are your life coaches. The protectors of the orthodoxy and dogma of the stories of the course and meaning of life.

"They are the gatekeepers of your destiny.

"Some of us hear the voices as thoughtful mentor, cherished parent, respected teacher, critic, coach, scorekeeper, grievance officer or my personal favorites, the criticizers-in-chief: oughta, shoulda, coulda and woulda.

"Some of us hear the voices of gods, devils and monsters beckoning us to do unspeakable things—as if we needed a devil to make us do them.

"The more responsible among us accept the voices as their own critiquing and second-guessing them, usually after it's too late to be helpful or constructive.

"The voices might be useful instead of distressing if their observations were made just prior to the miscalculation or mistake.

"Then there is our old friend anxiety. It's just that nagging visceral feeling that something is wrong.

"Anxiety isn't even civil enough to speak up and identify the problem.

"It is helpful in dealing with these distractions to remember that our stories [about the course and meaning of life] are idealized scripts and texts—the gold standard.

"How can you possibly achieve the gold standard without scorekeepers?"[4]

Agency in Life Can't Be Achieved Without Knowing the Stories of the Want-to-Bes and the Stories of the How-to-Bes

"Want-to-Bes" are the stories of the range of things we want out of life, pitfalls to avoid, and things that we believe make us feel good about being alive.

Want-to-Bes usually revolve around things like: family, career, respect, self-esteem, self-respect, peace of mind, happiness, fulfillment and success,

---

[4] *Without Stories, There is No Universe, Existence, Reality or You*, at pages 36, 37.

recognition, status, friendship, education, financial security, power, influence, *etc*.

Pick your poison.

Compare notes with family and friends.

It amazes me that most of us seem to want the same things out of life.

I guess it shouldn't.

We're all caught up in the same Story.

"How-to-Bes" are stories of how to achieve Want-to-Bes.

How-to-Bes stories are the step-by-step instructions that map the roads to that pie in the sky.

They are the blueprints and instructions that chart the rights-of-way to dreams and goals.

They are the mind's maps to success.

Here's the rub.

Although everybody is well versed in the Want-to-Bes, few of us know the stories of how to achieve the Want-to-Bes.

To gain Agency in life, it is imperative that you know or learn the How-to-Bes stories from others, your own research, or if you must, write them yourself.

It is impossible to attain Agency in life if you don't know the How-to-Bes instruction stories needed to achieve your Want-to-Bes.

Associate with, watch, study, and seek the advice of people you know who seem to have found pathways to their dreams. Emulate them.

Accept that nothing can be achieved without knowing the instructions that map the pathway from here to there.

Don't underestimate the value of trial and error in writing your own How-to-Bes instruction stories.

The Pathways to Agency

Now to the levers of Agency.

You might want to begin the Agency quest by quieting those noisy, unhelpful voices in your head.

You need a clear mind for the quest.

Understand that the stories about everything in the Story of Life crystallized as *idyllic* visions of the thing imagined.

Borrowing once more from *Without Stories*:

"The stories [about the course and meaning of life] tell us where we should be and what we should be doing at every point in our lives to attain the good life idealized in our stories about it.

"The stories tell us about our lot in life; what a good marriage looks like; what a successful career looks like; the acceptable way of acting and presenting ourselves; what an attractive person looks like; what a good person will and will not do, *etc.*

"Those voices are just your measuring sticks.

"They let you know how well you're doing on your journey through life and whether you are on track.

"The voices are scorekeepers and nothing more, even though their assessments may be laden with painful emotions."[5]

It seems to me that the first hurdle in taming the voices is remembering that they are your mind's way of tracking and scoring your character's performance and achievements against the proscriptions and prescriptions sanctioned in the Story of Life.

By the way, they are *your* voices even though to many they come across as someone else's—like, say,

---

[5] *Without Stories, There is No Universe, Existence, Reality, Or You,* at pages 37, 38.

a critical parent, or maybe a thoughtful mentor, or favorite teacher, or the voice of scripture, or big brother, or some other favored gaslighter; or maybe they are the sirens of some forbidden pleasure.

Too often, what the voices have to say is monumentally silly.

Here are of few of my favorites:

- What a slob you are.
- You aren't controlling your weight.
- You're not being given the respect that you deserve.
- You are a bad person.
- You're so boring.
- Nobody loves you.
- At the snail's pace you're moving, you aren't going to amount to anything.
- Everybody is out to get you.
- The deck is stacked against you.
- It's your fault.
- Face it, you're a loser.

Although scorekeeping should be instructive, the problem with the voices is that they rarely have anything constructive, positive or helpful to say.

Even though you feel the sting of their criticisms, the voices are the mind's way of keeping score on your progress, and nothing more.

My suggestions for dealing with the voices?

When the clatter begins to overwhelm, don't follow the voices into the rabbit hole—*mea culpa, mea culpa, mea culpa.*

Tell the voices that they are not being helpful and to "shut up."

Reasoning with the voices is a waste of time.

But give it a try if you must.

Counsel the voices that they are not very helpful with their nagging negativity and incessant bugging about things over which you have little or no control like your weight, your bank balance, that vacation that you don't have money for, your bad relationships, your failure at love, your stupidity, *etc.*

Didn't work, did it.

Then move on.

* * *

Now to the practical.

You can only feel alive if you secure a seat at the table of the Story of Life.

After all, the Story is the only game in town.

If you don't have a seat at the table, you're dead.

Agency in the performance of your bits in life cannot be achieved unless you accept that everything you do, feel and experience is the result of you slavishly emulating your character in the Story.

The Story of Life is not a decree from on high.

It's scary to even think such a thing.

It's blasphemy.

Have you braced yourself for the lightning strike?

No matter how real it feels, the Story we emulate is just a fairy tale.

It is nothing more than the historical prattle of mere mortals conjured in ignorance and desperation to create a survivable reality.

Since the reality that we experience is nothing more than conjurings, you should relieve yourself of the notion that your fate is anchored in divine truth.

Have you forgotten that mankind was cast out of the Garden of Eden?

Be fearless in your assault on the fairy tale that we are living.

Our challenge to it paves the road to fulfillment and redemption, not hell.

Five thousand years of written history counsels that redemption will not come from outside of us.

Redemption requires us to chart together new pathways in the Story that can quiet the demons of our making.

There can be no Agency in life without choice, i.e., until one sees or conceives options.

* * *

Here are some of my takes on the levers of Agency.

Since we experience life as community, we must understand how others see us; and make peace with ourselves if we fall short of expectations imposed by family and community.

Don't speculate. Ask others their opinion of your character in the Story.

It may seem frightening, but remind yourself that you are impacted by the opinions of others whether they are expressed to you or not.

Better yet, take the time to pay attention to the way others treat you. Actions do speak the loudest.

Watching is the key to understanding what others make of us.

It may turn out to be a painful exercise.

That's the way it has been for me, painful.

The worst part is realizing that, mostly, others are not paying much attention at all.

They are too busy doing their thing.

In a real sense, each of us is the center of the Universe.

It's impossible to become the person that fulfills our yearnings without setting our own expectations, insofar as we can.

Accept what you cannot change about your character's place in community.

Invest your energy and passion into changing the things you choose to change about your situation and have the power and wherewithal to do so.

Test each moment to determine for yourself whether you are being seduced by the scripts of the Story and its effect on you.

Ask yourself, is this really something I want, want to do, or want to be?

The standards and expectations that are sanctioned by the Story and that burden and oppress us and cause disappointment are also not anointed.

Change or walk away from standards and expectations that rob you of Agency in your life.

If you are disappointed with your character or situation, work to change them, or move on.

What you believe to be your destiny can be overcome by finding and exercising choices for your character; even if the choices are limited or you have to create them.

Take time to figure out what you want and what you don't want to do or be; and then chase after it or stay clear of it.

Choose what you want, not what your character is supposed to want. Focus your time and energy on the things you choose to want.

Emotions are the spice and perfume of existence.

Savor them; but don't be seduced by them. Resist their addictive swagger and their ability to overwhelm reason.

Take note of the power and range of your emotions and question whether the fever you feel is displaced.

Recognize and take notice of the parts and scripts that are available and unavailable to your character in the Story; but don't be corseted by them.

Be instructed by the resistance you sense in others when they feel that your character has crossed lines that circumscribe "your place" in family and community.

If you have no say in setting expectations for yourself, you do yourself a disservice by embracing feelings of disappointment because you fail to achieve what is expected.

You can't be wrong where there is no choice; you can't be judged guilty without choice.

Disavow a commitment to the zero-sum mentality that justifies ends above means.

It is hard to be victimized if you resist playing the victim.

Spend time comparing notes with others on things that are important to you. This is a good way to gain perspective on your lot in life.

If your character is part of an oppressed group, form alliances with others in the group and together discover mythical, magical stories of your group's past, present and future that elevate your kind.

Form alliances of the disenfranchised to establish franchise.

Nurture positive stories about your character and kind and reject negative ones.

Respect others and learn their Story and their place in it so that you can explain to them who you are and what you want in the language of scripts that *they* embrace and understand.

Use the power of stories to redefine your place and role in community.

Your paths to access are written in your parts and roles in community; rewrite the scripts that don't serve your interests.

Be aware that the reason you repeat the same mistakes over and over isn't because you are a bad or stupid person.

It's because the mistakes are the perseverations of the scripts that you're trapped in. They will always end the same way.

The way out of cycles of failure and disappointment is to learn or chart new pathways and look for and adopt alternative scripts with different endings.

Disappointment is the residue of failing to live up to expectations that may not be ones that you would choose if you perceived a choice.

Expand your vision of what is possible for your character, and pursue roles, parts and scripts that expand your reach in the Story, rather than limiting yourself to those scripted for your avatar.

Craft your own pathways.

Dispense with guilt, revenge, justice and blame.

They are your shackles.

The Story is a community enterprise rather than an individual enterprise.

The Story fixes and stabilizes community and our places in it.

Recognize the importance of listening to others and observing their appraisals and takes on life.

Compare notes with others whenever you can. It's a good way to get your bearings in the Story.

In my view, you cannot achieve Agency in life without transparent connections to others.

To really connect, commune and gain insight into another person's take on the Story—beyond the fleeting power of social convention, histrionics and hormones—you have to accept that others' interpretation of the Story of Life and their place in it may not be the same or even similar to yours.

You can't learn about yourself without comparing your views with others.

You can glean others' take on life by watching what they do and by listening to what they say as they interact with you and others.

Pursue others' perspectives with an open mind.

Compare and contrast and suspend judgment.

Recognize that all of us are ensnared and seduced by the parts of the Story that are embraced by our particular families and clans.

Recognize that all of us deem our own takes on the Story as *the* real and consequential.

Be aware that the antithetical scripts of "the others" are seen as heresy and are disbelieved, rejected or ignored.

Each of us has the Agency to alter or change our roles, parts and scripts in the Story.

But to do so, we have to step out of character and hover above the Story to see a way out of its bondage.

The progenitors' Story is the survivable reality that they conjured to gain a toehold on existence and consciousness, and nothing more.

The Story is not of our making.

It charts the destiny of the ignorant.

Keep in mind while pursuing the pathways to Agency that the only real purpose of the Story that was passed down generations was to create, anchor and stabilize a survivable reality and to imagine reasons to go on living.

It is just a fairy tale.

Together, we can craft the Story of Life as any reality that we dream.

Epilogue

Agency is achieved in life by mindfully manipulating and adjusting the scripts and plots of the fairy tale bequeathed to us by the progenitors.

That requires us to not allow ourselves to be seduced and overwhelmed by their Story; and requires us to not allow ourselves to be dragged down plotlines slavishly emulating parts and reciting the speeches of our characters, even when they diminish and destroy our humanity.

The progenitors' Story chronicles the pathways out of darkness and trumpets the course and meaning of life.

We experience life as we emulate our parts in the Story imagined by the progenitors.

We are performers in the dramas that they imagined and projected on three-dimensional landscapes and dreamscapes of their making.

Over the millennia, our lives have been scripted down to the minutest detail.

As an example, we greet each other with a plethora of canned pleasantries, followed-up with chit-chat and small talk, also canned, i.e., scripted.

We experience life within the bubble of the plots and scripts set out in the progenitors' fairy tale.

But, to the point, the bounty of our legacy is that it is our toehold on existence and self-consciousness, and that a story can be altered, or new ones written.

Altering the Story changes the experience of life.

All we need do is tweak the themes, plots and gambits of the Story and our parts in them.

We don't have to play the game of life as it has been written in the Story.

Pick up the quill and reimagine the Story; or at least claim the prerogatives of prophet or pundit, and critique and demand edits to the scripts.

Become the masters of fate.

Rewrite the themes, scripts and our parts in the Story of Life.

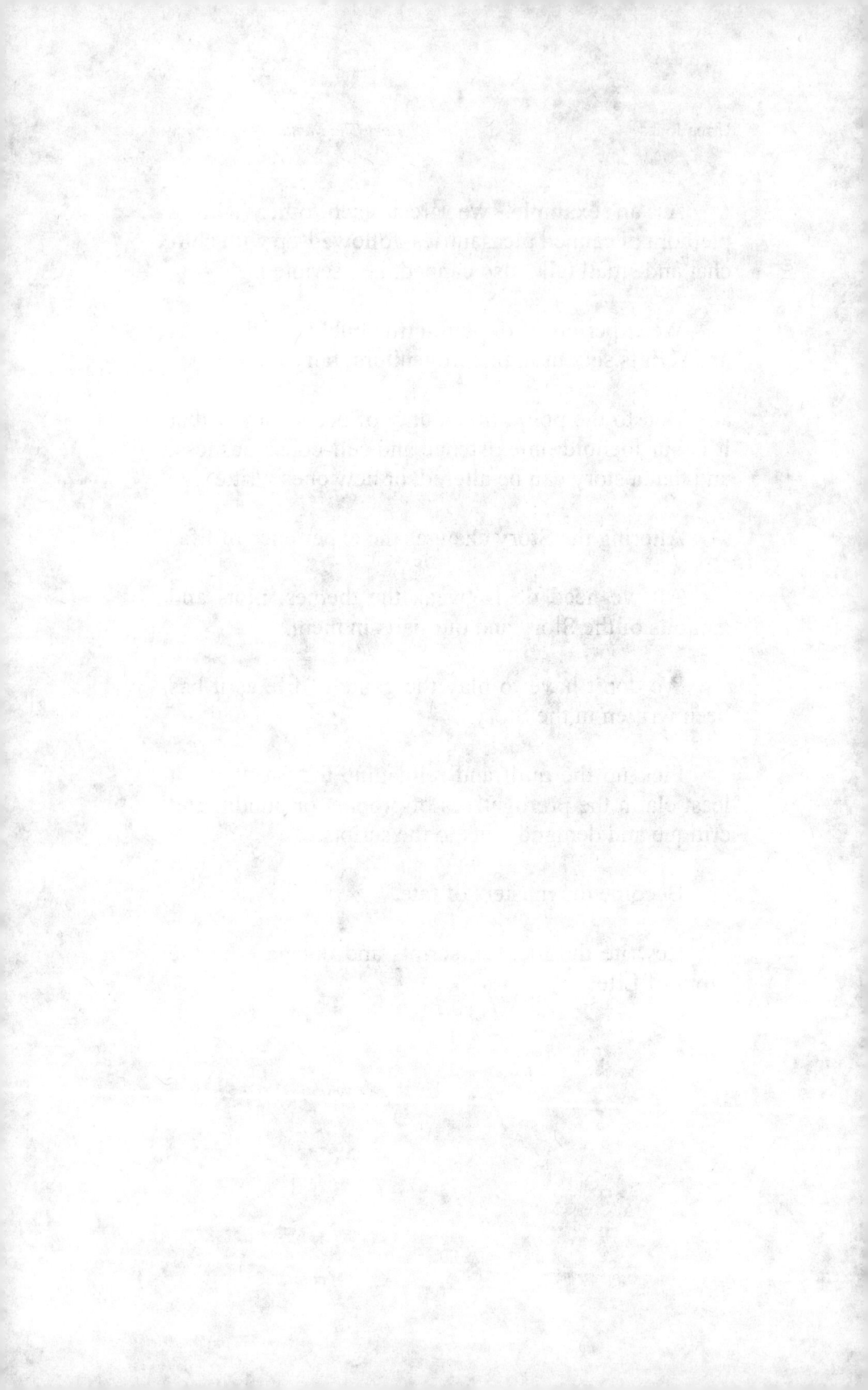

About the Author

Urrea Jones served as a public school teacher before practicing law for more than thirty years, first as a Los Angeles County Deputy County Counsel, and then in private practice representing public school districts.

He served in the United States Army, Vietnam.

He holds a bachelor's degree in the social sciences, a master's degree in sociology, and a Juris Doctor.

About the Book

In this book I consider the implications of accepting the inescapable truth about life.

The truth?

Everything in life is experienced and lived as stories.

Try thinking about anything, including yourself, without calling to mind or imagining a jumble of stories and vignettes about it.

Nothing exists without stories about it—not even you or me.

All that is knowable and known to us was conjured by the progenitors over millennia as the Story of Life.

This is the Story that gives direction and meaning to our lives.

The life that we experience is not anointed.

Because nothing can exist without stories describing the how, what, when, where and why of it, that means that existence, reality, consciousness and self, in short, *everything* at its core, is just our stories about it.

The Story is the brick and mortar of community and us.

Agency in life can be achieved by accepting that what we experience as life is just a concocted Story, and as such, it can be altered or rewritten to make our lives better.